CW01467203

ENGLAND'S LITERARY LANDMARKS

FIFTEEN MUST-SEE SITES

CHRISTY NICHOLAS

GREEN DRAGON PUBLISHING

Copyright © 2025 Christy Nicholas
Photography © 2025 by Christy Nicholas
Cover art © 2025 by Christy Nicholas
Internal design © 2025 by Green Dragon Publishing

All rights reserved. No part of this book may be reproduced in any form or by any electronic or mechanical means including information storage and retrieval systems, except in the case of brief quotations embodied in critical articles or reviews, without permission in writing from its publisher, Green Dragon Publishing.

The characters and events portrayed in this book are fictitious or are used fictitiously. Any similarity to real persons, living or dead, is purely coincidental and not intended by the author.

All brand names and product names used in this book are trademarks, registered trademarks, or trade names of their respective holders. Green Dragon Publishing is not associated with any product or vendor in this book.

Published by Green Dragon Publishing
Beacon Falls, CT
www.GreenDragonArtist.com

Table of Contents

Introduction
Bath (Jane Austen)
Bowness-on-Windermere (Beatrix Potter)
Bristol (Angela Carter)
Canterbury (Geoffrey Chaucer)
Chawton (Jane Austen)
Dorset (Thomas Hardy and Enid Blyton)
East Sussex (A. A. Milne and Virginia Woolf)
Haworth (Brontë Sisters)
London (Charles Dickens)
Oxford (J. R. R. Tolkein and C. S. Lewis)
Stratford-upon-Avon (William Shakespeare)
The Isle of Wight (Sir Alfred Lord Tennyson)
The Lake District (William Wordsworth)
Whitby (Bram Stoker)
Yorkshire (Ted Hughes and Sylvia Plath)
Conclusion
Thank You
About the Author

Introduction

England's literary heritage is as rich and diverse as the country itself, offering a tapestry of stories that span centuries and genres. From the grandeur of Shakespeare's birthplace to the quiet corners where iconic poets found their muse, England's literary landmarks invite travelers to step into the very settings that inspired some of the world's greatest works.

Whether you're a fan of classic novels, a lover of poetry, or a seeker of the places where history and imagination meet, England holds the keys to literary adventures.

In this guide, we'll explore fifteen must-visit literary landmarks that have shaped the nation's cultural and literary landscape. These sites not only honor the lives and works of England's most celebrated writers, but they also offer a glimpse into the places that sparked their creativity.

Whether wandering through the cobblestone streets of Oxford, standing in the shadow of the Brontë parsonage, or enjoying the peace of a country garden that inspired Wordsworth, you'll find that the stories of England are still alive and waiting to be discovered.

Join us as we journey through the pages of history and literature, where every landmark tells a story, and every visit brings the past to life.

On a practical note, for any opening times and entry fees, these are subject to change, so please check before visiting to avoid disappointment.

THE LAKE DISTRICT   WHITBY

SCARBOROUGH / YORKSHIRE

HAWORTH

YORKSHIRE

STRATFORD-UPON-AVON

OXFORD   LONDON

BRISTOL

CHAWTON

BATH   CAMBRIDGE

DORSET   EAST SUSSEX

THE ISLE OF WIGHT

Bath
(Jane Austen)

Background Information

Jane Austen (1775–1817) lived in Bath from 1801 to 1806, and the city profoundly influenced her novels, particularly *Northanger Abbey* and *Persuasion*.

Though Austen herself was ambivalent about Bath, describing it with both charm and criticism, the city provides a rich backdrop for her works and insights into Regency-era society.

Her experiences in Bath shaped her observations on social climbing, matchmaking, and the lives of genteel women, which feature prominently in her literature.

Literary Quotes

"They arrived in Bath. Catherine was all eager delight;—her eyes were here, there, everywhere, as they approached its fine and striking environs, and afterwards drove through those streets which conducted them to the hotel." — *Northanger Abbey* (1817)

"She recollected that a day or two before she had, unthinkingly, thrown down her pelisse on reaching home, and found it in the same place afterwards." — *Persuasion* (1818)

Key Jane Austen Sites in Bath

Jane Austen Centre
- **Location:** 40 Gay Street, Bath BA1 2NT
- **Description:** This immersive museum explores Austen's life and her time in Bath, featuring period costumes, interactive exhibits, and a wax figure of Jane Austen created using historical descriptions.
- **Must-See Features:** The Regency Tea Room, where visitors can enjoy afternoon tea, and exhibits about Austen's time in Bath.

Assembly Rooms and Fashion Museum
- **Location:** Bennett Street, Bath BA1 2QH
- **Description:** The grand Assembly Rooms, once a hub of social life in Austen's day, appear in *Northanger Abbey* and *Persuasion*. The adjacent Fashion Museum houses Regency-era attire.
- **Must-See Features:** The Ballroom, Tea Room, and period costume displays.

Sydney Gardens
- **Location:** Sydney Place, Bath BA2 6NT
- **Description:** The gardens near Austen's former home (4 Sydney Place) were a popular leisure spot, mentioned in her letters.
- **Must-See Features**: Serpentine canals, historic bridges, and a tranquil retreat for Austen fans.

Gravel Walk
- **Location:** Between Royal Crescent and Queen Square
- **Description:** A romantic pedestrian path where Anne Elliot and Captain Wentworth reconnect in *Persuasion*.
- **Must-See Features:** Panoramic views and a peaceful stroll through Regency-era Bath.

Bath Abbey & Pump Room
- **Location:** Abbey Churchyard, Bath BA1 1LT

- **Description:** A focal point in Austen's time, the Pump Room was a fashionable meeting place and features in *Northanger Abbey*.
- **Must-See Features:** Historic interior, live classical music, and traditional Bath spa water tasting.

Short Walking Route

- **Start:** Jane Austen Centre (Gay Street)
- Walk to **Assembly Rooms** (5-minute walk)
- Continue to **Bath Abbey** and **Pump Room** (10-minute walk)
- Stroll along **Gravel Walk** to **Royal Crescent** (15-minute walk)
- End at **Sydney Gardens** and **4 Sydney Place** (10-minute walk)

Visiting Information

- **Opening Hours:** Varies by site; Jane Austen Centre typically open 10 AM–5 PM
- **Days of Operation:** Most sites open daily
- **Entry Fees:**
  - Jane Austen Centre: £13.50 (adults), £6.50 (children)
  - Assembly Rooms: Free; Fashion Museum entry may have fees

- Pump Room: Free entry, but afternoon tea is chargeable
- **Accessibility:** Most sites have wheelchair access; Gravel Walk has uneven surfaces
- **Best Time to Visit:** Spring and autumn for fewer crowds; September for the Jane Austen Festival
- **What to Bring:** Comfortable walking shoes, light layers, Regency attire (optional for festival events!)

Literary Festivals & Events

- **Jane Austen Festival (September):** A 10-day event featuring Regency dances, costumed promenades, and author talks.
- **Bath Literature Festival (March):** Includes Austen-related panels and readings.

Nearby Attractions

- **⊠ e Roman Baths:** Explore Bath's ancient heritage.
- **Royal Crescent & ⊠ e Circus:** Iconic Georgian architecture.
- **Pulteney Bridge:** One of the most picturesque locations in Bath.

Further Reading

- *Northanger Abbey* and *Persuasion* by Jane Austen
- *Jane Austen at Home* by Lucy Worsley
- *A Visitor's Guide to Jane Austen's England* by Sue Wilkes

Bath is one of the best places to step into the world of Jane Austen, offering a blend of history, literature, and Regency charm.

Bowness-on-Windermere
(Beatrix Potter)

Background Information

Beatrix Potter (1866–1943) is one of the most beloved children's authors and illustrators, best known for *The Tale of Peter Rabbit* and other stories featuring charming animal characters inspired by the English countryside.

Potter had a deep connection to the Lake District, where she lived and worked, drawing inspiration from its landscapes for her iconic illustrations.

Her dedication to conservation helped preserve much of the region through her contributions to the National Trust.

Literary Quotes

"Peter gave himself up for lost, and shed big tears; but his sobs were overheard by some friendly sparrows, who flew to him in great excitement, and implored him to exert himself." – The Tale of Peter Rabbit (1902)

"The hedgehog laughed and wagged her head—I can hear her now, with her cap on the back of her head." – The Tale of Mrs. Tiggy-Winkle (1905)

Key Beatrix Potter Sites in Bowness-on-Windermere

☒ e World of Beatrix Potter Attraction

- **Location:** Crag Brow, Bowness-on-Windermere, LA23 3BX
- **Description:** An interactive experience bringing Potter's characters to life with immersive exhibits, animatronics, and recreations of scenes from her books.
- **Must-See Features:**
    - The Peter Rabbit Garden, which features plants and scenes from the stories.
    - The themed exhibition showcasing life-sized figures of Jemima Puddle-Duck, Mrs. Tiggy-Winkle, and more.

- The Beatrix Potter Tea Room, offering themed treats.

Hill Top Farm (Near Bowness-on-Windermere)
- **Location:** Near Sawrey, Ambleside, LA22 0LF (4 miles from Bowness-on-Windermere)
- **Description:** Beatrix Potter's former home, preserved as she left it, with many original furnishings and personal items.
- **Must-See Features:**
  - The study where Potter wrote many of her famous tales.
- The beautiful cottage garden that inspired *The Tale of Tom Kitten*.
  - Original sketches and letters from Potter's life.

St. Martin's Church
- **Location:** Church Street, Bowness-on-Windermere, LA23 3DG
- **Description:** A historic church visited by Beatrix Potter, offering a peaceful retreat and a glimpse into the town's heritage.
- **Must-See Features:**
  - The stained glass windows.
  - The surrounding gardens and scenic views of Lake Windermere.

Windermere Lake Cruises
- **Location:** Bowness Pier, Bowness-on-Windermere, LA23 3HQ
- **Description:** A scenic cruise on Lake Windermere, offering views of landscapes that inspired Potter's illustrations.
- **Must-See Features:**
    - Various cruise options, including a round trip to Near Sawrey.
    - Stunning views of the Lake District's rolling hills and historic sites.

Short Walking Route

- **Start:** The World of Beatrix Potter Attraction
- Walk to **St. Martin's Church** (5-minute walk)
- Stroll along **Bowness Bay** for scenic lake views (10-minute walk)
- Board a **Windermere Lake Cruise** to **Near Sawrey** (30-minute boat ride)
- Visit **Hill Top Farm** (short bus or taxi from the ferry landing)

Visiting Information

- **Opening Hours:** Varies by site; World of Beatrix Potter typically 10 AM–5 PM
- **Days of Operation:** Most sites open daily

- **Entry Fees:**
    - World of Beatrix Potter: £9.50 (adults), £5.00 (children)
    - Hill Top Farm: £15.00 (adults), £7.50 (children), free for National Trust members
    - Windermere Cruises: Prices vary (£10–£20 depending on route)
- **Accessibility:** The World of Beatrix Potter is wheelchair accessible; Hill Top has some uneven terrain.
- **Best Time to Visit:** Spring and autumn for fewer crowds; July for the Beatrix Potter Birthday Celebration.
- **What to Bring:** Comfortable shoes, light rain jacket, and a camera for capturing literary landscapes.

Literary Festivals & Events

- **Beatrix Potter Birthday Celebration** (July): Special events at the World of Beatrix Potter and Hill Top Farm.
- **Windermere Literary Festival** (September): Features author talks and children's storytelling sessions.

Nearby Attractions

- **⬛ e Lake District Visitor Centre at Brockhole:** A great spot for gardens and outdoor activities.
- **Blackwell, ⬛ e Arts & Crafts House:** A stunning example of early 20th-century design.
- **Wray Castle:** A National Trust site linked to Beatrix Potter's childhood holidays.

Further Reading

- *The Tale of Peter Rabbit* and other Beatrix Potter stories
- *Beatrix Potter: A Life in Nature* by Linda Lear
- *At Home with Beatrix Potter: The Creator of Peter Rabbit* by Susan Denyer

Bowness-on-Windermere offers an enchanting literary journey through the world of Beatrix Potter, making it a must-visit destination for fans of her timeless tales.

BOWNESS ON
WINDERMERE

Bristol
(Angela Carter)

Background Information

Angela Carter (1940–1992) was a bold and imaginative writer known for her magical realism, feminist themes, and gothic storytelling. She spent part of her formative years in Bristol, studying English at the University of Bristol in the early 1960s.

The city's rich history, maritime legacy, and eccentric atmosphere influenced her fiction, particularly *Shadow Dance* (1966), her debut novel set in a dystopian version of Bristol.

Literary Quotes

"This city I had chosen to live in ... its streets and squares and circuses, black and gold and ochre and raw brick red, impressed themselves upon me with an increasing intensity." – Angela Carter on Bristol
"Marianne saw her own reflection staring back at her from a dirty mirror in the corridor, but it was not her reflection." – Shadow Dance

Key Angela Carter Sites in Bristol

⊠ e University of Bristol

- **Location:** Tyndall Avenue, Bristol BS8 1TH
- **Description:** Angela Carter studied here from 1960 to 1963, an experience that shaped her intellectual development and early writing.
- **Must-See Features:**
    - The Arts and Social Sciences Library, where Carter spent much of her time reading.
    - The Wills Memorial Building, an iconic landmark with stunning Gothic architecture.

⊠ e Red Lodge Museum

- **Location:** Park Row, Bristol BS1 5LJ

- **Description:** A historic Elizabethan house with an eerie and atmospheric quality that mirrors Carter's gothic narratives.
- **Must-See Features:**
  - The Great Oak Room, known for its dark wood paneling and intricate carvings.
  - The secret gardens, offering a tranquil escape in the heart of the city.

St. Nicholas Market
- **Location:** Corn Street, Bristol BS1 1JQ
- **Description:** One of the oldest markets in Bristol, evoking the bohemian and eclectic vibe found in *Shadow Dance*.
- **Must-See Features:**
  - Unique vintage shops and bookstalls.
  - The Glass Arcade, filled with quirky cafes and independent traders.

Bristol Docks & Harbourside
- **Location:** Bristol BS1 5UH
- **Description:** A site linked to Carter's fascination with maritime culture and the dark undercurrents of human nature in her stories.
- **Must-See Features:**
  - The M Shed Museum, which explores Bristol's maritime and industrial history.

- o The historic pubs along King Street, reminiscent of the settings in *Shadow Dance*.

Short Walking Route

- **Start:** The University of Bristol (Tyndall Avenue)
- Walk to ⊠ e **Red Lodge Museum** (10-minute walk)
- Continue to **St. Nicholas Market** (10-minute walk)
- Stroll through **Bristol Docks & Harbourside** (15-minute walk)
- End at **M Shed Museum** (10-minute walk)

Visiting Information

- **Opening Hours:** Varies by site; most museums open 10 AM–5 PM
- **Days of Operation:** Most sites open daily except for some museums, which close on Mondays
- **Entry Fees:**
  - o The Red Lodge Museum: Free entry
  - o M Shed Museum: Free entry
  - o St. Nicholas Market: Free access
- **Accessibility:** Most sites are wheelchair accessible; some historic buildings may have limited access

- **Best Time to Visit:** Spring and autumn for fewer crowds; October for a gothic-themed experience
- **What to Bring:** Comfortable shoes, light jacket, and a notebook for literary inspiration

Literary Festivals & Events

- **Bristol Festival of Ideas (May):** Features discussions on literature, philosophy, and feminism, often including Carter's work.
- **Bristol Literary Festival (October):** Showcases author talks, workshops, and readings related to gothic and feminist literature.

Nearby Attractions

- **Bristol Cathedral:** A stunning medieval site with gothic architecture.
- **SS Great Britain:** A historic ship offering insight into Bristol's maritime legacy.
- **Arnolῥhi Arts Centre:** A hub for contemporary literature, art, and performance.

Further Reading

- *Shadow Dance* by Angela Carter
- *The Bloody Chamber and Other Stories* by Angela Carter

- *Angela Carter: A Biography* by Edmund Gordon

Bristol's rich literary and historical landscape offers an evocative setting for exploring Angela Carter's work and inspirations, making it a must-visit destination for fans of her dark and imaginative fiction.

BRISTOL

Canterbury
(Geo. rey Chaucer)

Background Information

Geoffrey Chaucer (c. 1343–1400) is known as the "Father of English Literature" and is best remembered for The Canterbury Tales, a collection of stories told by a diverse group of pilgrims traveling to Canterbury Cathedral.

His work provides a vivid snapshot of medieval society and has had a lasting impact on English literature. Canterbury remains an essential destination for literary travelers tracing the route of his famous pilgrims.

Literary Quotes

"Whan that Aprill with his shoures soote, The droghte of March hath perced to the roote..."
— *The Canterbury Tales (late 14th century)*

"And specially, from every shires ende Of Engelond, to Caunterbury they wende, The hooly blisful martir for to seke, That hem hath holpen whan that they were seeke."
— *The Canterbury Tales (late 14th century)*

Key Geoffrey Chaucer Sites in Canterbury

Canterbury Cathedral
- **Location:** Cathedral House, 11 The Precincts, Canterbury CT1 2EH
- **Description:** The destination of Chaucer's pilgrims and one of England's most significant religious sites.
- **Must-See Features:**
  - The shrine of Saint Thomas Becket, the martyred Archbishop who inspired the pilgrimage in *The Canterbury Tales.*

- The beautiful medieval stained glass windows depicting pilgrimages and historical figures.
- The cloisters and crypt, offering a glimpse into medieval ecclesiastical life.

⊠ e Canterbury Tales Visitor Attraction

- **Location:** St. Margaret's Street, Canterbury CT1 2TG
- **Description:** A live storytelling experience that brings Chaucer's tales to life through costumed actors and interactive exhibits.
- **Must-See Features:**
  - Life-sized reconstructions of scenes from *The Canterbury Tales*.
  - Engaging medieval-themed storytelling performances.
  - A replica medieval inn setting, evoking the pilgrims' journey.

⊠ e Westgate Towers

- **Location:** St. Peter's Street, Canterbury CT1 2BQ
- **Description:** A historic medieval gatehouse that the pilgrims would have passed through upon entering Canterbury.
- **Must-See Features:**

- o Climb to the top for panoramic views of Canterbury.
- o Explore the museum showcasing Canterbury's medieval history.
- o Walk along the ancient city walls.

Eastbridge Hospital
- **Location:** 25 High Street, Canterbury CT1 2BD
- **Description:** A medieval pilgrim's hospital offering insight into the hospitality provided to travelers on their way to Canterbury Cathedral.
- **Must-See Features:**
  - o The Pilgrims' Chapel, where weary travelers once prayed.
  - o The medieval refectory and dormitory.
  - o The tranquil courtyard garden.

Short Walking Route

- **Start:** The Canterbury Tales Visitor Attraction
- Walk to **Westgate Towers** (5-minute walk)
- Continue to **Eastbridge Hospital** (5-minute walk)
- Proceed to **Canterbury Cathedral** (10-minute walk)
- End with a visit to ⊠ e **Buttermarket**, a medieval square with historic charm

Visiting Information

- **Opening Hours:** Canterbury Cathedral typically 9 AM–5 PM, but closing time may vary
- **Days of Operation:** Most sites open daily
- **Entry Fees:**
    - Canterbury Cathedral: £17.00 (adults), £11.50 (children)
    - The Canterbury Tales Visitor Attraction: £10.00 (adults), £8.00 (children)
    - Westgate Towers: £4.00 (adults), £2.00 (children)
    - Eastbridge Hospital: £4.00 (adults), £3.00 (children)
- **Accessibility:** Most sites are wheelchair accessible, though some historic buildings have uneven surfaces. Some locations, such as Eastbridge Hospital, may have uneven floors.
- **Best Time to Visit:** Spring and autumn for fewer crowds; April for Chaucer-themed events.
- **What to Bring:** Comfortable walking shoes, a rain jacket, and a copy of *The Canterbury Tales* for reference.

Literary Festivals & Events

- **Canterbury Festival (October):** A cultural celebration featuring literature, music, and theatre.
- **Medieval Pageants (Summer):** Reenactments of pilgrim journeys and medieval storytelling events.

Nearby Attractions

- **St. Augustine's Abbey:** A UNESCO World Heritage Site showcasing early Christian history.
- **⊠ e Beaney House of Art & Knowledge:** A fascinating mix of museum exhibits and rare books.
- **Canterbury Roman Museum:** A journey into Canterbury's ancient past.

Further Reading

- *The Canterbury Tales* by Geoffrey Chaucer
- *Chaucer: A European Life* by Marion Turner
- *The Life of Geoffrey Chaucer: A Critical Biography* by Derek Pearsall

Canterbury offers an unparalleled opportunity to step into the world of Geoffrey Chaucer and experience the medieval pilgrimage that inspired one of English literature's greatest works.

CANTERBURY

Chawton
(Jane Austen)

Background Information

Jane Austen (1775–1817) is one of England's most celebrated novelists, known for her keen social observations and timeless works such as Pride and Prejudice, Sense and Sensibility, and Emma. Chawton, a small village in Hampshire, is where Austen spent the last eight years of her life and where she wrote or revised many of her most famous novels.

Today, Chawton remains a pilgrimage site for Austen fans eager to step into the world that inspired her stories.

Literary Quotes

"There is nothing like staying at home for real comfort." – Emma

"Ah! There is nothing like staying at home for real comfort." – Emma

"A woman, especially, if she have the misfortune of knowing anything, should conceal it as well as she can." – Northanger Abbey

Key Jane Austen Sites in Chawton

Jane Austen's House
- **Location:** Winchester Road, Chawton, Hampshire GU34 1SD
- **Description:** The house where Austen lived from 1809 to 1817, now a museum dedicated to her life and works.
- **Must-See Features:**
  - Austen's writing table where she penned her greatest novels.
  - Personal belongings, including her jewelry and letters.

- o The garden Austen often walked in for inspiration.

Chawton House
- **Location:** Chawton, Alton, Hampshire GU34 1SJ
- **Description:** The home of Jane Austen's brother, Edward Austen Knight, now a research library focusing on early women's literature.
- **Must-See Features:**
  - o The Great Hall, where Austen would have dined with her family.
  - o The extensive collection of rare books by female authors.
  - o Beautiful grounds that inspired Austen's depictions of country estates.

St. Nicholas Church
- **Location:** Chawton, Alton, Hampshire GU34 1SJ
- **Description:** The parish church associated with the Austen family, where Austen's mother and sister are buried.
- **Must-See Features:**
  - o Austen family memorials and gravestones.
  - o Tranquil churchyard perfect for quiet reflection.

Short Walking Route

- **Start:** Jane Austen's House
- Walk to **St. Nicholas Church** (5-minute walk)
- Continue to **Chawton House** (10-minute walk)
- Stroll along **Chawton Village** to take in the picturesque thatched cottages and countryside

Visiting Information

- **Opening Hours:**
  - Jane Austen's House: Typically 10 AM–5 PM (varies by season)
  - Chawton House: Typically 10 AM–4 PM (varies by season)
  - St. Nicholas Church: Open daily, with varying hours
- **Days of Operation:** Most sites open daily, though some have seasonal closures.
- **Entry Fees:**
  - Jane Austen's House: £12.00 (adults), £6.00 (children)
  - Chawton House: £10.00 (adults), £5.00 (children)
  - St. Nicholas Church: Free
- **Accessibility:** Most sites are wheelchair accessible, though some historic buildings have uneven flooring.

- **Best Time to Visit:** Spring and summer for gardens in bloom; autumn for fewer crowds.
- **What to Bring:** Comfortable shoes for walking, an umbrella for unpredictable weather, and a copy of *Pride and Prejudice* for a literary touch.

Literary Festivals & Events

- **Jane Austen Regency Week (June):** A celebration featuring period costumes, talks, and dances.
- **Chawton House Literary Festival (Autumn):** Events focused on women's literature and history.

Nearby Attractions

- **Winchester Cathedral:** Austen's final resting place.
- **Alton:** A charming market town with additional Austen connections.
- **Gilbert White's House & Gardens:** A historic home dedicated to the famous naturalist.

Further Reading

- *Pride and Prejudice* by Jane Austen
- *Jane Austen at Home* by Lucy Worsley
- *The Real Jane Austen: A Life in Small Things* by Paula Byrne

Chawton offers an intimate glimpse into the world of Jane Austen, making it a must-visit destination for literature lovers.

Dorset
(☒ omas Hardy and
Enid Blyton)

Background Information

Thomas Hardy (1840–1928) was one of England's most renowned novelists and poets, best known for his vivid depictions of rural life and the fictional region of Wessex, based on his native Dorset. His novels, including Tess of the d'Urbervilles, Far from the Madding Crowd, and The Mayor of Casterbridge, capture the landscape, traditions, and hardships of 19th-century rural England.

Enid Blyton (1897–1968) was one of the most prolific and beloved children's authors of the 20th century. Her adventure-filled stories, including The Famous Five, The Secret Seven, and The Magic Faraway Tree series, have enchanted generations of young readers. Blyton's works are often set in idyllic countryside locations, reflecting her love for nature and the English landscape. Her ability to create engaging mysteries and memorable characters has ensured her books remain timeless classics.

Literary Quotes

Thomas Hardy: "Happiness was but the occasional episode in a general drama of pain." – The Mayor of Casterbridge (1886) "We two kept house, the past and I." – Poems of 1912-13 "A little cloud of music flies / Above the sown and reaped, / It is the tone to memory / Of minstrels long since passed to rest." – Under the Greenwood Tree (1872)

Enid Blyton: "Somehow, you'll have to manage to be brave—and I know you will!" – The Famous Five "There's nothing like a good adventure to set you up!" – The Secret Seven "Magic always seems impossible until it's done." – The Magic Faraway Tree

Key Hardy Sites in Dorset

Hardy's Cottage
- **Location:** Higher Bockhampton, near Dorchester, Dorset DT2 8QJ
- **Description:** The birthplace and early home of Thomas Hardy, this charming thatched cottage is where he wrote *Far from the Madding Crowd*.
- **Must-See Features:**
  - The room where Hardy wrote his early novels.
  - The picturesque garden that inspired much of his pastoral imagery.
  - Original furnishings and exhibits detailing his early life.

Max Gate
- **Location:** Alington Avenue, Dorchester, Dorset DT1 2AB
- **Description:** The home designed by Hardy himself, where he lived for over 40 years and wrote *Tess of the d'Urbervilles* and *Jude the Obscure*.
- **Must-See Features:**
  - Hardy's study, preserved with original writing materials.
  - The gardens where he and his first wife, Emma, often walked.

- o   Insights into his later life, including his work as an architect.

Stinsford Church
- **Location:** Stinsford, near Dorchester, Dorset DT2 8PT
- **Description:** Hardy's heart is buried here beside his first wife, Emma, while his ashes rest in Westminster Abbey.
- **Must-See Features:**
  - o   Hardy family graves.
  - o   Connection to *Under the Greenwood Tree*, as Stinsford Church inspired Mellstock Church in the novel.

Enis Blyton's Dorset
- **Location:** Swanage, Corfe Castle, and Studland Bay
- **Description:** Blyton frequently visited Dorset, and the region inspired many locations in her Famous Five series, including Kirrin Island and the castles and coastlines central to her stories
- **Must-See Features:**
  - o   **Corfe Castle,** believed to be the inspiration for Kirrin Castle
  - o   **Swanage Railway**, reminiscent of the steam trains in her adventure stories

- o ☒ e scenic **Dorset coastline,** which appears in many of her works.

Short Walking Route

For ☒ omas Hardy fans:
- **Start:** Max Gate
- Walk to **Dorchester Corn Exchange** (15-minute walk)
- Continue to **Stinsford Church** (20-minute walk)
- End at **Dorset County Museum** (10-minute walk)

For Enid Blyton fans:
- **Start:** Corfe Castle
- Walk to **Swanage Railway** (20-minute walk)
- End at **Studland Bay** (30-minute scenic walk)

Visiting Information

Hardy's Cottage
- **Opening Hours:**
  - o Hardy's Cottage: Open seasonally, typically March–October, 10 AM–4 PM. Check before visiting.
  - o Max Gate: Open year-round, 11 AM–5 PM

- **Days of Operation:** Varies by site; check National Trust websites for updates.
- **Entry Fees:**
    - Hardy's Cottage: ~£8.00 (adults), discounts for families and National Trust members.
    - Max Gate: ~£8.00 (adults), similar discounts available.
- **Accessibility:**
    - Hardy's Cottage has limited access due to its historic nature.
    - Max Gate is more accessible with ramps and assistance available.
- **Best Time to Visit:** Spring and summer for pleasant weather and gardens in bloom; autumn for fewer crowds.
- **What to Bring:** Comfortable walking shoes, a raincoat, and a copy of *Far from the Madding Crowd* for inspiration.

Corfe Castle
- **Opening Hours:** The castle is usually open 10am – 5pm during the summer and 10am – 4pm in the winter. Check before visiting.
- **Days of Operation:** Varies by site; check National Trust websites for updates.
- **Entry Fees:** £12.00 (adults), discounts for children and families available.

- **Accessibility:** Corfe Castle has uneven terrain and limited accessibility.
- **Best Time to Visit:** Spring and summer for pleasant weather and gardens in bloom; autumn for fewer crowds.
- **What to Bring:** Comfortable walking shoes, a raincoat, and a copy of *The Famous Five* for inspiration.

Literary Festivals & Events

- **⬚ omas Hardy Festival (Dorchester, July):** A week-long festival with lectures, readings, and guided tours.
- **Hardy Country Walking Tours (Year-Round):** Led by literary experts covering key sites and their significance.
- **Enid Blyton Day** (Swanage, August): A celebration of Blyton's works with storytelling, reenactments, and themed activities.

Nearby Attractions

- **Lulworth Cove & Durdle Door:** Stunning coastal scenery featured in Hardy's poetry.
- **Corfe Castle:** A historic site believed to have inspired parts of *The Trumpet-Major*.

- **Tolpuddle Martyrs Museum:** A social history museum exploring themes of rural hardship, similar to those in Hardy's novels.
- **Martyrs Museum:** A social history museum exploring themes of rural hardship, similar to those in Hardy's novels.

Further Reading

- *Far from the Madding Crowd* by Thomas Hardy
- *Tess of the d'Urbervilles* by Thomas Hardy
- *Thomas Hardy: The Time-Torn Man* by Claire Tomalin
- *The Life and Work of Thomas Hardy* by Thomas Hardy (autobiographical)
- *The Famous Five* series by Enid Blyton
- *Enid Blyton: A Biography* by Barbara Stoney

Exploring Hardy Country and Enid Blyton's Dorset offers an immersive experience into the worlds of two literary greats. Whether walking the pastoral landscapes of Hardy's Wessex or uncovering the adventure-filled locations of Blyton's stories, visitors can step into the pages of English literary history.

East Sussex (A.A. Milne and (B. Virginia Woolf)

Background Information

Virginia Woolf (1882–1941) and A.A. Milne (1882–1956) were two of the most influential British writers of the 20th century, each leaving a lasting literary legacy. Woolf, a pioneering modernist, was known for her stream-of-consciousness style and feminist themes, while Milne, beloved for his Winnie-the-

Pooh stories, captured the innocence of childhood with whimsical charm.

Both authors had deep connections to the English countryside, finding inspiration in East Sussex. Woolf spent much of her life in Rodmell, where she wrote many of her greatest works, while Milne lived near Hartfield, drawing upon the picturesque Ashdown Forest to create the Hundred Acre Wood. Today, visitors can explore the landscapes and homes that shaped their literary worlds.

Literary Quotes

Virginia Woolf: "A woman must have money and a room of her own if she is to write fiction." – A Room of One's Own (1929)
"I am made and remade continually. Different people draw different words from me." – The Waves (1931)
"Against you I will fling myself, unvanquished and unyielding, O Death!" – The Waves (1931)
A.A. Milne: "You are braver than you believe, stronger than you seem, and smarter than you think." – Winnie-the-Pooh (1926)
"Sometimes the smallest things take up the most room in your heart." – Winnie-the-Pooh (1926)
"Weeds are flowers too, once you get to know them." – Winnie-the-Pooh (1926)

Key Literary Sites in East Sussex

Monk's House (Virginia Woolf)
- **Location:** Rodmell, Lewes, East Sussex BN7 3HF
- **Description:** Virginia and Leonard Woolf's country home, now preserved by the National Trust.
- **Must-See Features:**
    - Woolf's writing lodge in the garden where she worked on many of her novels.
    - Personal belongings, books, and photographs that offer insights into her life.
    - Beautiful gardens where Woolf often walked and found inspiration.

Charleston Farmhouse (Virginia Woolf)
- **Location:** Firle, Lewes, East Sussex BN8 6LL
- **Description:** The home of Woolf's sister, Vanessa Bell, and a key gathering place for the Bloomsbury Group.
- **Must-See Features:**
    - Vibrant murals and paintings by Bell and Duncan Grant.
    - The studio spaces where the Bloomsbury artists worked.

- o Gardens designed to reflect the artistic and intellectual spirit of the group.

Pooh Corner & Ashdown Forest (A.A. Milne)
- **Location:** Hartfield, East Sussex TN7 4AE
- **Description:** The charming village of Hartfield and the surrounding Ashdown Forest served as the inspiration for the Hundred Acre Wood.
- **Must-See Features:**
  - o Pooh Corner, a delightful shop and tearoom dedicated to A.A. Milne and Winnie-the-Pooh.
  - o The iconic Poohsticks Bridge, where visitors can play the beloved game from the stories.
  - o Walking trails through Ashdown Forest, including sites such as the Enchanted Place and Galleon's Lap.

Short Walking Routes

Virginia Woolf's River Ouse Walk
- **Start:** Monk's House
- **Walk to:** St. Peter's Church, Rodmell, where Leonard Woolf is buried (5-minute walk)
- **Continue to:** Virginia Woolf's River Ouse Walk (15-minute walk)

- **End at:** Lewes, a historic town with Woolf connections (accessible via short drive or bus)

Winnie-the-Pooh Trail in Ashdown Forest
- **Start:** Pooh Corner, Hartfield
- **Walk to:** Poohsticks Bridge (15-minute walk)
- **Continue to:** The Enchanted Place (20-minute walk)
- **End at:** Galleon's Lap, a scenic viewpoint loved by Milne (15-minute walk)

Visiting Information

- **Opening Hours:**
  - Monk's House: March–October, 11 AM–5 PM (varies by season)
  - Charleston Farmhouse: April–October, 10 AM–5 PM (varies by season)
  - Pooh Corner: Open year-round, typically 10 AM–4 PM
- **Entry Fees:**
  - Monk's House: £9.00 (adults), £4.50 (children)
  - Charleston Farmhouse: £16.00 (adults), £8.00 (children)
  - Ashdown Forest: Free access, donations welcome

- **Best Time to Visit:**
    - Spring and summer for blooming gardens; early autumn for fewer crowds.
    - Ashdown Forest is beautiful year-round, but autumn offers stunning foliage.

Literary Festivals & Events

- **Charleston Festival (May):** A celebration of literature, art, and ideas inspired by the Bloomsbury Group.
- **Small Wonder Short Story Festival (Autumn):** A festival dedicated to the art of short fiction, held at Charleston.
- **Winnie-the-Pooh Day (January 18):** Events at Pooh Corner to celebrate A.A. Milne's birthday.

Nearby Attractions

- **Lewes Castle & Museum:** A Norman castle with stunning views of the South Downs.
- **Seven Sisters Cli. s:** Breathtaking coastal scenery reminiscent of Woolf's descriptions of England's landscapes.
- **Glyndebourne Opera House:** A world-famous venue for classical music lovers.
- **Bateman's:** The former home of Rudyard Kipling, another literary great of Sussex.

Further Reading

Virginia Woolf:
- *To the Lighthouse*
- *A Room of One's Own*
- *Virginia Woolf: A Biography* by Hermione Lee

A.A. Milne:
- *Winnie-the-Pooh*
- *The House at Pooh Corner*
- *The Red House Mystery* (Milne's lesser-known detective novel)

East Sussex offers a deeply personal glimpse into the lives of Virginia Woolf and A.A. Milne, making it an essential destination for literary enthusiasts of all ages.

EAST SUSSEX

Haworth
(Brontë Sisters)

Background Information

Haworth, a small village in West Yorkshire, England, is renowned for being the birthplace and home of the Brontë sisters: Charlotte, Emily, and Anne. The Brontë family lived in the parsonage at Haworth from 1820 to 1861.

The moorland setting, with its wild and often gloomy atmosphere, deeply influenced the sisters' works, which include Jane Eyre, Wuthering Heights, and The Tenant of Wildfell Hall. Their novels, poetry, and tales of love, loss, and rebellion, set against the rugged Yorkshire landscape, have cemented the Brontës as pillars of English literature.

Charlotte Brontë's Jane Eyre is a powerful reflection of self-resilience, while Emily's Wuthering Heights is celebrated for its intense exploration of obsessive love and its gothic elements. Anne's The Tenant of Wildfell Hall explores themes of marital discord and the rights of women. The Brontë sisters' works have had a lasting influence on literature, inspiring generations of writers and readers.

Literary Quotes

"Happiness was but the occasional episode in a general drama of pain." – Jane Eyre (1847)
"We were born to strive and struggle, and though we may seem in the end to have gained little, we may have gained something of greater value." – Shirley (1849)

"A wild, dark, stormy night; and the rain beat fiercely on the windows of the room where I sat alone." – Wuthering Heights (1847)

Key Brontë Sisters Sites in Haworth

Brontë Parsonage Museum

- **Location:** Haworth, West Yorkshire
- **Description:** The family home where the Brontë sisters wrote their famous novels, now a museum showcasing their lives, manuscripts, and personal artifacts.
- **Must-See Features:** Charlotte's writing desk, Emily's piano, and the study where their father, Patrick Brontë, worked.

⊠ e Parsonage Garden
- **Location:** Adjacent to the Brontë Parsonage Museum
- **Description:** A peaceful garden reflecting the Brontës' love for nature, offering scenic views of the surrounding moorland.
- **Must-See Features:** Picturesque landscapes and seasonal flora that inspired their works.

⊠ e Brontës' Personal Belongings
- **Location:** Brontë Parsonage Museum
- **Description:** A collection of original manuscripts, letters, and personal items belonging to the sisters.
- **Must-See Features:** Charlotte's writing desk and Emily's portrait of her dog.

⊠ e Wuthering Heights Experience
- **Location:** Top Withens, near Haworth

- **Description:** A remote farmhouse believed to be the inspiration for Wuthering Heights, set in the dramatic Yorkshire moors.
- **Must-See Features:** Stunning moorland views and the atmospheric ruins linked to Brontë's novel. *It is commonly debated whether Top Withens is the true inspiration for Wuthering Heights. While it is a popular visitor site linked to the novel, Emily Brontë never explicitly confirmed this location as the model for her fictional setting. There's no definitive proof connecting the farmhouse to Wuthering Heights.*

Short Walking Route

- **Start: Brontë Parsonage Museum**
- **Walk to: St. Michael** and **All Angels Church,** where the Brontë family is buried (5-minute walk)
- **Continue to:** The wild moors that inspired their novels (10-minute walk)
- **End at: Top Withens,** a remote farmhouse ruin linked to Wuthering Heights (1.5-mile scenic hike)

Visiting Information

- **Opening Hours:** Daily, 10:00 AM - 5:00 PM (Check for specific holiday hours)
- **Days of Operation:** Open every day except Christmas Day and Boxing Day.
- **Address:** Brontë Parsonage Museum, Church Street, Haworth, BD22 8DR, West Yorkshire, UK.
- **Entry Fees:** £9 for adults, £4 for children (aged 5-16), £7.50 for seniors/students. Special tours or events may have additional fees.
- **Accessibility:** The museum is wheelchair accessible with a lift to the first floor and ramp access at the entrance. The terrain around the village and moors may be difficult for those with mobility issues, so comfortable walking shoes are recommended.
- **Best Times to Visit:** Spring and autumn offer fewer crowds and the best views of the surrounding moors. The museum is particularly atmospheric in winter when the moors are shrouded in mist and the fireplaces in the parsonage are lit.
- **What to Bring:** Comfortable walking shoes, especially if you plan to explore the nearby moors, and a camera for the stunning landscapes. Dress in layers, as the weather can be unpredictable in the Yorkshire moors.

Literary Festivals & Events

- **Brontë Society Events:** Throughout the year, the Brontë Parsonage Museum hosts a variety of events, including author talks, themed tours, and readings from the Brontë family's works.
- **Brontë Festival of Women's Writing (September):** This annual event celebrates women writers with talks, performances, and discussions, attracting both established and emerging authors.

Nearby Attractions

- **St. Michael and All Angels Church:** Visit the church where the Brontë family is buried, located just a short walk from the parsonage. The churchyard offers a peaceful reflection on the Brontës' legacy.
- **Keighley and Worth Valley Railway:** A heritage railway, often featuring themed train rides for literature lovers, running through the beautiful Yorkshire countryside.
- **Bronte Waterfall and Top Withens:** For more adventurous literary travelers, these nearby spots provide stunning views and a deeper connection to the wild landscapes that inspired the Brontë novels.

- **☒ e Keighley and Worth Valley Railway:** A scenic train ride through the picturesque Yorkshire countryside.

Further Reading
- *The Brontë Sisters by Catherine O'Flynn:* A fascinating look into the lives and works of the three sisters.
- *The Brontës: Wild Genius on the Moors by Juliet Barker:* A comprehensive biography of the Brontë family and their connection to the Haworth moors.
- *Wuthering Heights by Emily Brontë:* No visit to Haworth is complete without reading or revisiting the Brontë classic set in the haunting Yorkshire moors.

Haworth offers an unforgettable experience for any literary traveler. It's a place where the spirit of the Brontë sisters still lingers in the air, and the stories they wrote come to life through the wild landscapes and historic sites that inspired them.

HAWORTH

London
(Charles Dickens)

Background Information

Charles Dickens, one of the greatest novelists of the Victorian era, spent much of his life in London, and the city profoundly influenced his work. Born in 1812, Dickens experienced the hardships of early life, particularly during his childhood when his family faced financial difficulties.

His experiences in the slums and bustling streets of London became central themes in novels such as

Oliver Twist, Bleak House, Great Expectations, and A Tale of Two Cities. Dickens' vivid characters and sharp social commentary often highlight the stark contrasts between the wealthy elite and the impoverished working class, and London serves as both a setting and a character in many of his works.

Literary Quotes

Quote from Dickens: "It was the best of times, it was the worst of times, it was the age of wisdom, it was the age of foolishness…"
— A Tale of Two Cities (1859)

"There is a wisdom of the head, and a wisdom of the heart." – Hard Times (1854)

Key Dickens Sites in London

Charles Dickens Museum
- **Location:** 48 Doughty Street, London
- **Description:** Housed in Dickens' former residence, this Georgian townhouse is where he wrote *Oliver Twist* and *Nicholas Nickleby*. The museum showcases manuscripts, personal letters, and portraits offering a fascinating glimpse into his life.
- **Must-See Features:** Dickens' writing desk, original manuscripts, and period furnishings.

Dickens' Home at 1 Devonshire Terrace
- **Location:** 1 Devonshire Terrace, London
- **Description:** Dickens lived here from 1839 to 1844 and wrote *A Christmas Carol* within its walls. Though now a private residence, it remains an important stop for Dickens enthusiasts.
- **Must-See Features:** The exterior and historical significance as the birthplace of *A Christmas Carol.*

⊠ e Old Curiosity Shop
- **Location:** Portsmouth Street, London
- **Description:** A charming 16th-century shop believed to have inspired Dickens' novel *The Old Curiosity Shop*. Though its literary connection is debated, the building remains a fascinating landmark. Tthere is a long-standing debate about its authenticity as the inspiration for the shop in his novel. The connection is largely speculative.
- **Must-See Features:** The quaint, timber-framed structure and its ties to Dickensian London.

⊠ e Royal Court ⊠ eatre
- **Location:** Sloane Square, London
- **Description:** A theatre Dickens frequently visited, known for staging productions of his plays and adaptations of his novels.

- **Must-See Features:** The historic auditorium and ongoing performances celebrating Dickens' literary legacy.

Short Walks

Charles Dickens Walking Tour (Bloomsbury & Holborn)
- **Start: Charles Dickens Museum**
- **Walk to: 1 Devonshire Terrace** (10-minute walk)
- **Continue to:** ⊠ e **Old Curiosity Shop** (10-minute walk)
- **End at:** Former site of **Fleet Prison** (15-minute walk)

Dickensian London Walk
- **Start: Sa. ron Hill** (approx. 20-minute walk from starting point)
- **Walk to: Marshalsea Prison** site (15-minute walk)
- **Continue to:** Locations from **Oliver Twist, Great Expectations**, and **A Tale of Two Cities** (20-minute walk)
- **End at:** Key landmarks associated with Dickens' works throughout the 3-mile walk

Visiting Information

- **Opening Hours:**
  Charles Dickens Museum: Daily, 10:00 AM - 5:00 PM
  Closed on Christmas Eve, Christmas Day, and Boxing Day.
- **Days of Operation:** Open every day except for major holidays.
- **Address:** Charles Dickens Museum, 48 Doughty Street, London, WC1N 2LX, UK
- **Costs:**
  Charles Dickens Museum: £9.50 for adults, £4.50 for children (6-16), £7.50 for seniors. Discounts available for students and group tours. Special events and exhibitions may have an additional fee.
- **Accessibility:**
  The Charles Dickens Museum is wheelchair accessible via a ramp at the entrance. However, as the building is a historic townhouse, there are stairs to access some areas, which may be difficult for those with mobility issues. It's recommended to check for updates on access before visiting.
- **Best Times to Visit:**
  The museum is less crowded during the winter months, especially January and February. For a quieter experience and to avoid crowds, visit in the mornings on weekdays.

- **What to Bring:** Comfortable walking shoes, as many of the literary sites require walking or walking tours through various parts of London. Also, bring a camera to capture the rich history around you.

Literary Festivals & Events

- **Dickensian Christmas Festival (December):** Held annually in December, this festival celebrates Dickens' legacy with readings, costume displays, and festive activities. Visitors can enjoy a Dickensian-themed Christmas market, as well as performances from local theater companies.
- **London Literature Festival (October):** This event features author talks, panel discussions, and literary performances, with frequent references to Dickens and his legacy in the events lineup.

Nearby Attractions

- **⬜ e British Museum:** Just a short walk from the Charles Dickens Museum, the British Museum offers an extensive collection of artifacts, including items from Dickens' era.
- **Covent Garden:** A lively area filled with street performers, shops, and restaurants, Covent Garden also has a rich literary history. Nearby,

you can visit Drury Lane, which Dickens mentioned in many of his works.

- ⊠ e **Museum of London:** For those interested in the historical context of Dickens' novels, the Museum of London offers exhibitions on Victorian London, including a look at the squalid conditions of the slums Dickens wrote about in *Oliver Twist* and *Bleak House.*
- **Southbank Centre:** A cultural hub for the arts, this area regularly hosts literary events, and you may find Dickens-themed performances and exhibitions throughout the year.

Further Reading

- *Dickens: A Life* by Claire Tomalin: A detailed and compelling biography of Dickens, exploring both his personal and professional life.
- *The Life and Adventures of Nicholas Nickleby* by Charles Dickens: One of Dickens' most famous works, capturing the hardships and triumphs of young Nicholas as he navigates the corrupt world around him.
- *Charles Dickens: A Critical Study* by G.K. Chesterton: This classic book offers insight into Dickens' life and works, written by one of his greatest admirers.

Exploring the literary landmarks of Charles Dickens' London offers a fascinating journey through the life of one of the greatest storytellers in English literature. Whether you're walking in his footsteps or visiting the very buildings that inspired his iconic novels, London remains a city deeply intertwined with Dickens' legacy.

Oxford
(J.R.R. Tolkien and
C.S. Lewis)

Background Information

Oxford, renowned for its prestigious university, is a key location in the lives and works of two literary giants, J.R.R. Tolkien and C.S. Lewis. Both authors spent significant parts of their lives in Oxford, and it is in this city that they formed the friendships and intellectual foundations that led to the creation of their most famous works.

J.R.R. Tolkien (1892-1973), best known for The Hobbit and The Lord of the Rings, was a professor of Anglo-Saxon at Oxford University. His love of languages, mythology, and the natural world, all shaped the detailed world-building in his writings. Tolkien's deep connection to Oxford, with its ancient colleges and tranquil surroundings, influenced much of his fictional landscapes.

C.S. Lewis (1898-1963), best known for The Chronicles of Narnia, was a professor of Medieval and Renaissance English at Oxford. His works, which blend Christian allegory with fantasy, were heavily inspired by his Oxford experiences and friendships, particularly with Tolkien. Together, the two formed part of the literary group known as the Inklings, which met regularly to discuss literature and share ideas.

Literary Quotes

Quote from J.R.R. Tolkien: "The road goes ever on and on / Down from the door where it began."
— The Fellowship of the Ring (1954)

"All that is gold does not glitter, / Not all those who wander are lost."
— *The Fellowship of the Ring (1954)*

Quote from C.S. Lewis: "We are what we believe we are."
— *The Chronicles of Narnia: Prince Caspian (1951)*

Key Sites in Oxford

⬚ e Eagle and Child Pub
- **Location:** St Giles', Oxford
- **Description:** A historic pub where the Inklings, a literary group including J.R.R. Tolkien and C.S. Lewis, met regularly to discuss their works. The pub retains its cozy atmosphere and features memorabilia related to the writers.
- **Must-See Features:** The "Rabbit Room," where the Inklings gathered, and displays honoring Tolkien and Lewis.

Merton College (Tolkien's College)
- **Location:** Merton Street, Oxford
- **Description:** Tolkien served as a professor here, and his time at Merton College played a significant role in his literary career. The college gardens and surrounding areas are believed to have inspired elements of *The Lord of the Rings*.

- **Must-See Features:** The medieval architecture, picturesque gardens, and Tolkien's academic connection.

Magdalen College (C.S. Lewis's College)
- **Location:** High Street, Oxford
- **Description:** C.S. Lewis was a fellow and lecturer at Magdalen College for many years. Its stunning architecture and gardens influenced his writing, including the *Chronicles of Narnia*. The nearby Deer Park evokes the landscapes described in his novels.
- **Must-See Features:** The Deer Park, cloisters, and rooms where Lewis taught and wrote.

⊠ e Bodleian Library
- **Location:** Broad Street, Oxford
- **Description:** One of the world's greatest libraries, the Bodleian houses rare manuscripts and letters from both Tolkien and Lewis. Its grand reading rooms provide insight into the literary world that shaped their works.
- **Must-See Features:** Original Tolkien and Lewis manuscripts and the historic Duke Humfrey's Library.

⊠ e Kilns (C.S. Lewis's Home)
- **Location:** Headington, Oxford

- **Description:** The former home of C.S. Lewis, where he wrote many of his works, including the *Narnia* series. Now a museum, the house offers a glimpse into his creative process and personal life.
- **Must-See Features:** Lewis's study, personal artifacts, and the surrounding woodland that inspired *The Chronicles of Narnia*.

Short Walks

Tolkien and Lewis Walking Tour
- **Start:** Eagle and Child Pub
- **Walk to:** Merton College (15-minute walk)
- **Continue to:** Magdalen College (10-minute walk)
- **End at:** Bodleian Library (15-minute walk)

⌧ e Oxford Literary Walk
- **Start:** Bodleian Library
- **Walk to:** Radcliffe Camera (5-minute walk)
- **Continue to:** Various college gardens and courtyards (15-minute walk)
- **End at:** Literary landmarks associated with Oxford authors, including Tolkien and Lewis (approx. 3-mile walk)

Visiting Information

- **Opening Hours:**
  - The Eagle and Child Pub: Daily from 11:00 AM - 11:00 PM.
  - Merton College: Open from Monday to Saturday, 10:00 AM - 5:00 PM.
  - Magdalen College: Open daily from 9:00 AM - 5:00 PM.
  - The Bodleian Library: Monday to Saturday, 9:00 AM - 5:00 PM (closed on Sundays).
  - The Kilns: Tours available by appointment only, Monday to Saturday (times vary).
- **Days of Operation:** Most sites are open throughout the year, with some closures during holidays.
- **Address:**
  - The Eagle and Child Pub: 49 St Giles', Oxford, OX1 3LU, UK
  - Merton College: Merton St, Oxford, OX1 4JD, UK
  - Magdalen College: High St, Oxford, OX1 4AU, UK
  - The Bodleian Library: Broad Street, Oxford, OX1 3BG, UK
  - The Kilns: Lewis Close, Headington, Oxford, OX3 8JD, UK
- **Costs:**

- o The Eagle and Child Pub: No entry fee, but food and drink are available for purchase.
- o Merton College: £5 for adults, free for Oxford students.
- o Magdalen College: £7 for adults, £4 for students and seniors.
- o The Bodleian Library: £10 for adults, £5 for students, free entry for Oxford University staff.
- o The Kilns: £7 for adults, £5 for students, with special rates for group tours.
- **Accessibility:** Most locations are accessible to those with mobility issues. However, Merton College and Magdalen College have some areas with uneven surfaces and steps. The Kilns has wheelchair access to some parts, but visitors should contact in advance for specific accessibility requirements.
- **Best Times to Visit:** Spring and early autumn are ideal for a quieter experience with fewer tourists. The summer months can get busy, especially around Oxford's graduation season.
- **What to Bring:** Comfortable walking shoes for the city walk, a camera for scenic shots of Oxford's historic colleges, and a jacket in case of unpredictable weather.

Literary Festivals & Events:

- **Oxford Literary Festival (March/April):** Held annually in Oxford, this festival brings together authors, scholars, and literary enthusiasts to discuss a wide range of topics. Events related to Tolkien and Lewis often feature prominently, with lectures, panel discussions, and readings.
- **Tolkien Society's Annual Conference (July):** A dedicated event for fans of J.R.R. Tolkien, where experts, academics, and fans gather to discuss Tolkien's work, life, and legacy.
- **C.S. Lewis Society Annual Lecture (November):** A lecture dedicated to the works and legacy of C.S. Lewis, often featuring prominent scholars of his writing.

Nearby Attractions

- **⊠ e Ashmolean Museum:** Oxford's museum of art and archaeology, which features collections spanning thousands of years of human history.
- **Christ Church College:** A stunning college in Oxford, famous for its architecture and also a filming location for the *Harry Potter* movies.
- **Pitt Rivers Museum:** A fascinating museum with exhibits on anthropology and archaeology, showcasing the cultures that influenced the

imagination of many writers, including Lewis and Tolkien.

Further Reading

- *J.R.R. Tolkien: A Biography* by Humphrey Carpenter: A definitive biography of Tolkien, exploring his life, career, and impact on modern literature.
- *C.S. Lewis: A Life* by Alister McGrath: A biography of C.S. Lewis that delves into his intellectual and spiritual journey.
- *The Oxford Inklings: Lewis, Tolkien, and Their Circle* by Humphrey Carpenter: A great introduction to the literary group that included Tolkien and Lewis, offering insight into their friendship and collaborative influence.

Oxford provides a literary pilgrimage that captures the essence of both J.R.R. Tolkien and C.S. Lewis. Visitors can explore the places where these authors lived, worked, and created some of the most beloved works in fantasy literature, while walking in the footsteps of the two writers who forever changed the literary landscape.

Stratford-upon-Avon (William Shakespeare)

Background Information

William Shakespeare (1564–1616) is widely regarded as the greatest playwright and poet in the English language, and his works have had a profound influence on literature, theater, and culture worldwide. Born in Stratford-upon-Avon, this market town is deeply intertwined with Shakespeare's life and legacy.

Known for his plays such as Romeo and Juliet, Macbeth, and Hamlet, Shakespeare's genius in crafting complex characters and exploring human emotions has made his works timeless. Stratford-upon-Avon remains one of the most significant literary destinations in the world, offering visitors a chance to walk in the footsteps of the Bard.

Literary Quotes

Quote from Hamlet: "To be, or not to be: that is the question."
— Hamlet (1600)

"Cowards die many times before their deaths; / The valiant never taste of death but once." — Julius Caesar (1599)

"Now is the winter of our discontent / Made glorious summer by this sun of York."
— Richard III (1593)

Key Shakespeare Sites in Stratford-Upon-Avon

Shakespeare's Birthplace
- **Location:** Henley Street, Stratford-upon-Avon
- **Description:** The half-timbered house where Shakespeare was born and spent his early years. Visitors can explore period-preserved rooms and

interactive exhibits that provide insight into his formative years and the Elizabethan era.

- **Must-See Features:** Shakespeare's childhood room, period furniture, and exhibits on his early life.

Anne Hathaway's Cottage

- **Location:** Shottery, Stratford-upon-Avon
- **Description:** The picturesque childhood home of Shakespeare's wife, Anne Hathaway. A short walk from the town center, this thatched cottage offers a glimpse into 16th-century rural life and Shakespeare's courtship of Anne.
- **Must-See Features:** The charming gardens, original Tudor furniture, and the romantic setting.

⊠ e Royal Shakespeare ⊠ eatre

- **Location:** Waterside, Stratford-upon-Avon
- **Description:** Home to the Royal Shakespeare Company (RSC), this renowned theatre stages world-class productions of Shakespeare's plays. Visitors can watch a performance or take a backstage tour.
- **Must-See Features:** Live Shakespearean productions, behind-the-scenes tours, and panoramic views from the theatre tower.

Hall's Croft

- **Location:** Old Town, Stratford-upon-Avon
- **Description:** The former home of Shakespeare's daughter, Susanna, and her husband, Dr. John Hall. The house contains exhibits about life in Shakespeare's time and 17th-century medical practices.
- **Must-See Features:** Period medical instruments, beautifully restored interiors, and a peaceful walled garden.

Shakespeare's New Place

- **Location:** Chapel Street, Stratford-upon-Avon
- **Description:** The site of Shakespeare's final home, where he lived for the last 19 years of his life. Though the house was demolished in the 18th century, the gardens and exhibits offer insight into his later years.
- **Must-See Features:** Sculptures inspired by Shakespeare's works, interactive exhibits, and tranquil gardens reflecting his legacy.

Short Walks

⊠ e Shakespeare Trail

- **Start:** Shakespeare's Birthplace
- **Walk to:** Anne Hathaway's Cottage (15-minute walk)

- **Continue to:** Hall's Croft (10-minute walk)
- **End at:** Royal Shakespeare Theatre (10-minute walk)

⊠ e River Avon Walk

- **Start:** Royal Shakespeare Theatre
- **Walk to:** Holy Trinity Church (15-minute walk)
- **End at:** Scenic views along the River Avon (approx. 1-mile walk)

Visiting Information

- **Opening Hours:**
  - Shakespeare's Birthplace: Open daily from 9:00 AM to 5:00 PM.
  - Anne Hathaway's Cottage: Open daily from 9:00 AM to 5:00 PM.
  - The Royal Shakespeare Theatre: Performance times vary depending on the schedule.
  - Hall's Croft: Open daily from 10:00 AM to 5:00 PM.
  - Shakespeare's New Place: Open daily from 10:00 AM to 5:00 PM.
- **Days of Operation:**

- All sites are open year-round, though the Royal Shakespeare Theatre has performances from March to December.
- **Address:**
  - Shakespeare's Birthplace: Henley Street, Stratford-upon-Avon, CV37 6QW, UK
  - Anne Hathaway's Cottage: Shottery, Stratford-upon-Avon, CV37 9HH, UK
- **Costs:**
  - Shakespeare's Birthplace: £17 for adults, £11 for children (5-17), £45 for a family ticket.
  - Anne Hathaway's Cottage: £13 for adults, £7 for children (5-17), £34 for a family ticket.
  - Royal Shakespeare Theatre: Ticket prices vary depending on the performance.
  - Hall's Croft: £9.50 for adults, £5 for children (5-17), £26 for a family ticket.
  - Shakespeare's New Place: £9.50 for adults, £5 for children (5-17), £26 for a family ticket.
- **Accessibility:** Most of the sites are wheelchair accessible, though some older buildings may have limited access. The Royal Shakespeare Theatre

and Shakespeare's Birthplace are both fully accessible.

- **Best Times to Visit:** Spring and early autumn offer milder weather and fewer crowds. Summer is peak tourist season, so expect larger crowds at key sites.

- **What to Bring:** Comfortable shoes for walking, especially for exploring the town's streets and gardens. An umbrella or rain jacket is recommended, as Stratford-upon-Avon can be rainy, especially in the autumn and winter months.

Literary Festivals & Events:

- ⬚ e Stratford-upon-Avon Literary Festival **(April):** An annual event that celebrates literature with a wide range of talks, workshops, and author readings. The festival often features Shakespearean themes and draws international authors and literary enthusiasts.

- **Shakespeare Birthday Celebrations (April):** A week-long celebration of Shakespeare's birthday, including parades, plays, and events throughout the town, culminating in a ceremonial wreath-laying at Shakespeare's grave in Holy Trinity Church.

- **⬜ e Royal Shakespeare ⬜ eatre Season (March–December):** The Royal Shakespeare Company puts on numerous Shakespeare plays and other classic works throughout the year. The theatre is also home to educational events, such as talks and exhibitions.

Nearby Attractions

- **Holy Trinity Church:** The final resting place of William Shakespeare. Visitors can pay their respects at his grave inside this beautiful parish church, which also features a memorial to the Bard.

- **Stratford Butterfly Farm:** A tropical indoor rainforest housing thousands of butterflies from around the world, providing a unique experience for nature lovers and families.

- **⬜ e Cotswolds:** Stratford-upon-Avon is a gateway to the Cotswolds, a region of picturesque villages, rolling hills, and charming countryside, perfect for a scenic escape after exploring the town's literary history.

Further Reading

- *Shakespeare: The Biography* by Peter Ackroyd: A detailed biography that delves into Shakespeare's life and work.

- *Shakespeare's Stratford* by David Milward: A comprehensive guide to the town of Stratford-upon-Avon and its connection to the life of the Bard.

- *The Life of William Shakespeare* by Sir Sidney Lee: A classic biography of the playwright, providing insight into his life and times.

- *The Oxford Handbook of Shakespeare* edited by Arthur F. Kinney: A scholarly work that explores the cultural, historical, and literary contexts of Shakespeare's works.

Stratford-upon-Avon offers a rich and immersive experience for literary tourists, allowing visitors to connect with the life and legacy of William Shakespeare in a town that has preserved its historical ties to the Bard for centuries. Whether attending a play, touring historic homes, or simply strolling through the charming streets, the town remains a living tribute to the genius of Shakespeare.

⊠ e Isle of Wight (Sir Alfred Lord Tennyson)

Background Information

Alfred, Lord Tennyson (1809-1892), one of England's most famous poets, spent the latter part of his life on the Isle of Wight, where he found both inspiration and solace. Best known for his narrative poems such as The Charge of the Light Brigade and Idylls of the King, Tennyson's works helped define Victorian poetry.

Tennyson was appointed Poet Laureate in 1850, a position he held for the rest of his life, and his poetry often reflected themes of nature, love, loss, and the human condition. His time on the Isle of Wight, particularly in the village of Freshwater, greatly influenced his writing, offering a tranquil setting amidst the island's natural beauty.

Literary Quotes

"The old order changeth, yielding place to new, / And God fulfils himself in many ways."
— *The Idylls of the King (1859)*

"'Tis better to have loved and lost / Than never to have loved at all."
— *In Memoriam (1850)*

Key Tennyson Sites on The Isle of Wight

Farringford House
- **Location:** Freshwater, Isle of Wight
- **Description:** Tennyson's home from 1853 until his death in 1892. The house and gardens have been carefully restored to reflect the poet's life and creative process. Visitors can explore Tennyson's personal belongings, manuscripts, and portraits.

- **Must-See Features:** The poet's study, original furnishings, and the beautiful gardens that inspired his work.

Tennyson Down
- **Location:** Near Freshwater, Isle of Wight
- **Description:** A breathtaking chalk ridge offering panoramic views of the island and sea. Tennyson frequently walked here, drawing inspiration for many of his poetic themes.
- **Must-See Features:** The stunning coastal views, walking trails, and the famous Tennyson Memorial.

St. Agnes' Church
- **Location:** Freshwater, Isle of Wight
- **Description:** The small, picturesque church where Tennyson worshipped. The site features a memorial to the poet and is also the final resting place of his wife, Emily, and other family members.
- **Must-See Features:** Tennyson's memorial plaque, historic stained-glass windows, and the tranquil churchyard.

Tennyson Memorial (Alfred Tennyson's Statue)
- **Location:** Tennyson Down, Isle of Wight

- **Description:** A striking statue of Tennyson stands atop the Down, overlooking the dramatic coastline. The monument commemorates the poet's deep connection to the landscape.
- **Must-See Features:** The imposing statue, scenic viewpoints, and walking trails leading to Freshwater Bay.

Short Walks

Tennyson Trail
- **Start:** Farringford House
- **Walk to:** Tennyson Down (30-minute walk)
- **Continue to:** Village of Freshwater (20-minute walk)
- **End at:** Farringford House (15-minute walk)

Freshwater Bay and Tennyson Down Circular Walk
- **Start:** Freshwater Bay
- **Walk to:** Tennyson Down (20-minute walk)
- **Continue to:** Tennyson Memorial (10-minute walk)
- **End at:** Freshwater Bay (15-minute walk)

Visiting Information

- **Opening Hours:**

- o Farringford House: Open to visitors from March to October, 10:00 AM – 5:00 PM. Last entry at 4:30 PM.
- o Tennyson Down and the Memorial: Open year-round for walking and exploration.
- **Days of Operation:** Farringford House is open Monday through Saturday (closed on Sundays during the off-peak season).
- **Address:** Farringford House, Freshwater, Isle of Wight, PO40 9PE, UK
- **Costs:**
  - o Farringford House: £8 for adults, £4 for children (5-16), free for children under 5.
  - o Tennyson Down and the Memorial: Free.
- **Accessibility:**
  - o Farringford House is partially accessible to those with mobility issues, but the upper floors may be difficult to reach. Please contact the house directly for further accessibility details.
  - o Tennyson Down has uneven terrain and may be challenging for visitors with mobility issues. A less demanding route is available through Freshwater Bay.
- **Best Times to Visit:** Spring and early autumn are ideal for fewer crowds and pleasant weather. The summer months can get busier, particularly around holiday weekends.

- **What to Bring:** Comfortable walking shoes, especially if exploring Tennyson Down or the Tennyson Trail. Bring layers of clothing, as weather conditions can change quickly, especially on the exposed hilltops. Don't forget your camera to capture the breathtaking views.

Literary Festivals & Events:

- **Isle of Wight Literary Festival (October):** A celebrated event held annually on the island, featuring talks, readings, and discussions by contemporary authors. Though not directly focused on Tennyson, the festival often highlights historical literary figures, including the poet.
- **Tennyson Day (August):** A celebration of Tennyson's life and works, this annual event is held at Farringford House. The day includes readings of his poems, historical talks, and a chance to explore the poet's home and grounds.

Nearby Attractions

- ⊠ e Needles: A famous natural landmark on the Isle of Wight, with striking white cliffs and dramatic views of the sea. Tennyson was known to have admired the Needles, and they are often depicted in his poetry.

- **Carisbrooke Castle:** A medieval castle that offers a fascinating history, including its role during the English Civil War. The castle grounds also provide beautiful views of the island.
- **Isle of Wight Coastal Path:** For those wanting to explore more of the island's stunning coastline, the Coastal Path offers dramatic views of the sea and cliffs, and provides access to many of the island's natural wonders.

Further Reading

- *Tennyson: A Biography* by Graham Dawson: A comprehensive biography of Alfred, Lord Tennyson, exploring his life, family, and literary legacy.
- *The Collected Poems of Alfred Lord Tennyson* (edited by Christopher Ricks): A definitive collection of Tennyson's works, including all his major poems.
- *Tennyson: To Strive, To Seek, To Find* by John Batchelor: A biography that delves deeply into Tennyson's time on the Isle of Wight and his lasting impact on poetry.

The Isle of Wight offers visitors a peaceful, picturesque setting that still resonates with the legacy of Alfred, Lord Tennyson. Whether exploring his home, walking the trails he loved, or simply enjoying the natural beauty that inspired him, this island remains a place of deep literary significance.

THE ISLE OF WIGHT

☒ e Lake District (William Wordsworth)

Background Information

William Wordsworth (1770–1850) was one of the leading figures of the Romantic movement, known for his deep connection to nature and innovative use of simple language in poetry.

His most famous works, including *Lines Composed a Few Miles Above Tintern Abbey* and *I Wandered Lonely as a Cloud*, were heavily inspired by the Lake District's breathtaking landscapes. Born in Cockermouth, Wordsworth spent much of his life in this picturesque region, finding in its hills, lakes, and valleys a source of spiritual renewal and poetic inspiration.

Literary Quotes

"I wandered lonely as a cloud / That floats on high o'er vales and hills." — I Wandered Lonely as a Cloud (1807)
"Come forth into the light of things, / Let Nature be your teacher." — The Tables Turned (1798)
"Though nothing can bring back the hour / Of splendor in the grass, of glory in the flower." — Ode on Intimations of Immortality (1807)

Key Wordsworth Sites in the Lake District

Dove Cottage & ⊠ e Wordsworth Museum
- **Location:** Grasmere, Lake District, Cumbria, LA22 9SH
- **Description:** Dove Cottage was Wordsworth's home from 1799 to 1808, where he wrote much of his most celebrated poetry. The adjacent Wordsworth Museum houses manuscripts, letters, and artifacts that bring his life and work into vivid detail.
- **Must-See Features:**
  - Wordsworth's writing room, where many of his poems were composed.

- o Dorothy Wordsworth's famous journals, which provide insights into their daily lives.
- o First editions of *Lyrical Ballads*, co-authored with Samuel Taylor Coleridge.
- o The charming cottage garden, a place of inspiration for his nature-themed poetry.

Rydal Mount & Gardens
- **Location:** Rydal, Lake District
- **Description:** Wordsworth's home from 1813 until his death in 1850, offering insight into his later years. The house is surrounded by beautiful gardens and overlooks Rydal Water, both of which heavily influenced his writing.
- **Must-See Features:**
  - o Landscaped gardens designed by Wordsworth himself.
  - o Stunning views of the surrounding countryside that inspired many of his later works.

St. Oswald's Church & Wordsworth's Grave
- **Location:** Church St, Grasmere, LA22 9SW
- **Description:** The final resting place of William Wordsworth, set in a peaceful churchyard near the River Rothay.
- **Must-See Features:**

- ○ Wordsworth's simple yet poignant gravestone.
- ○ The Wordsworth Daffodil Garden, a tribute to the poet's famous poem.

Grasmere Lake & The Surrounding Landscape

- **Location:** Grasmere, Lake District
- **Description:** The breathtaking scenery of Grasmere Lake and its surrounding hills provided endless inspiration for Wordsworth's poetry.
- **Must-See Features:**
  - ○ Walking trails along the lake and panoramic views of the fells.
  - ○ Landscapes that shaped *The Prelude* and *Tintern Abbey*.

Short Walking Routes

Wordsworth Walk

- **Start:** Dove Cottage
- **Walk to:** The Wordsworth Museum (next door)
- **Continue to:** St. Oswald's Churchyard (10-minute walk)
- **End at:** Grasmere Lake for a reflective stroll (5-minute walk)

Rydal Water & The Poet's Path

- **Start:** Rydal Mount

- **Walk to:** Rydal Water (15-minute walk)
- **Continue to:** Rydal Gardens, a picturesque spot that influenced Wordsworth's work (10-minute walk)
- **End at:** Views of the surrounding fells (10-minute walk)

Visiting Information

- **Opening Hours:**
    - *Dove Cottage & Museum:* Typically open daily, 10 AM–5 PM (seasonal variations apply)
    - *Rydal Mount:* Open from April to October, 11 AM–5 PM
- **Entry Fees:**
    - *Dove Cottage & The Wordsworth Museum:* £14.00 (adults), £8.00 (children), discounts available.
    - *Rydal Mount:* £7.00 (adults), £3.00 (children), £5.00 (seniors).
    - Discounted tickets available for joint entry to both sites.
- **Accessibility:**
    - Limited wheelchair access due to historic buildings; the museum is more accessible than Dove Cottage.
- **Best Time to Visit:**

- ○ Spring for Wordsworth's beloved daffodils; autumn for a quieter experience and stunning foliage.
- **What to Bring:** Comfortable walking shoes, a raincoat, and a notebook for poetry-inspired reflections.

Literary Festivals & Events

- **Wordsworth Grasmere Poetry Festival (Spring):** A celebration of Romantic poetry with readings, workshops, and talks.
- **Dove Cottage Poets (Year-Round):** Regular poetry readings and discussions held at the museum.

Nearby Attractions

- **Rydal Mount & Gardens:** Wordsworth's later home with stunning views.
- **Lake Windermere:** England's largest lake, offering boat tours and scenic walks.
- **Hill Top (Beatrix Potter's Home):** A short drive from the Lake District, this preserved home offers a glimpse into another beloved literary figure's life.

- **⬚e Heaton Cooper Studio:** A gallery showcasing artwork inspired by the Lake District's natural beauty.

Further Reading

- *The Prelude* by William Wordsworth
- *Lyrical Ballads* by William Wordsworth & Samuel Taylor Coleridge
- *Dorothy Wordsworth's Grasmere Journals* (providing a personal view of life at Dove Cottage)
- *Wordsworth: A Life* by Juliet Barker

Visiting the Lake District offers a unique opportunity to step into the world of one of England's greatest poets and experience the landscapes that fueled his creativity.

THE LAKE
DISTRICT

Whitby
(Bram Stoker)

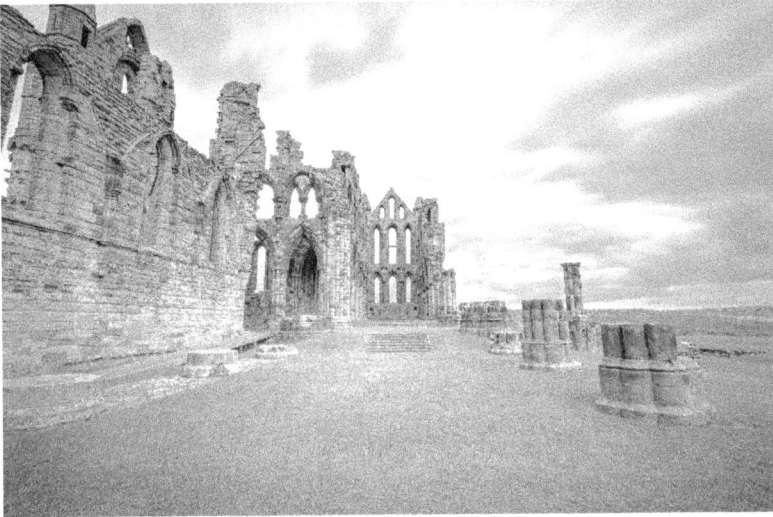

Background Information

Bram Stoker (1847–1912) is best known for writing Dracula, the iconic Gothic horror novel that has captivated readers for over a century. Although Stoker was born in Dublin, Ireland, it was during a visit to the coastal town of Whitby in 1890 that he found the inspiration for many of the supernatural elements in his novel.

Stoker's connection to Whitby is most notably tied to the dramatic landscapes, particularly the Whitby

Abbey ruins and the eerie cliffs, which helped inspire the vivid descriptions in Dracula.

Literary Quotes

"The very stone seemed to have a name, and the wind was howling like a wolf's cry." — Dracula (1897)

"Listen to them – the children of the night. What music they make!" — Dracula (1897)

Key Stoker Sites in Whitby

Whitby Abbey
- **Location:** Whitby, North Yorkshire
- **Description:** The haunting ruins of Whitby Abbey, perched high on a cliff overlooking the sea, served as a key inspiration for *Dracula*. In the novel, the abbey is where Count Dracula first arrives in England. The dramatic, crumbling structure and its vast cemetery set the Gothic tone for many of the novel's scenes.
- **Must-See Features:** The atmospheric ruins, stunning coastal views, and the connection to *Dracula*.

St. Mary's Churchyard
- **Location:** Next to Whitby Abbey
- **Description:** This eerie graveyard, with its weathered tombstones, plays a central role in

Dracula. It is the setting of a pivotal scene in which the ship's crew members bury a mysterious man who washes ashore.

- **Must-See Features:** The historic gravestones, Gothic ambiance, and panoramic views of Whitby.

☒ e 199 Steps
- **Location:** Leading from Whitby town to the abbey
- **Description:** These steep, winding steps are famously climbed by Jonathan Harker in *Dracula*. The journey to the top provides breathtaking views of the town and sea, adding to the novel's vivid sense of place.
- **Must-See Features:** The iconic steps, historical plaques, and spectacular vantage points.

☒ e Dracula Experience
- **Location:** Near Whitby Harbor
- **Description:** An interactive attraction that explores Whitby's role in *Dracula*, featuring exhibits, props, and artifacts related to the novel's characters and scenes.
- **Must-See Features:** The immersive displays, Gothic storytelling, and eerie atmosphere.

Whitby Harbour and the Old Town

- **Location:** Whitby, North Yorkshire
- **Description:** The narrow streets and historic harbor evoke the late 19th-century setting of *Dracula*. The harbor is where Dracula's ship, the *Demeter*, arrives in the novel, bringing the Count to English soil.
- **Must-See Features:** The picturesque harbor, historic buildings, and literary significance.

Short Walks

⊠ e Whitby Dracula Walk
- **Start:** Whitby Abbey
- **Walk to:** St. Mary's Churchyard (15-minute walk)
- **Continue to:** The 199 Steps (10-minute walk)
- **End at:** Whitby Harbour (10-minute walk)

Whitby Abbey to St. Mary's Church
- **Start:** Whitby Abbey
- **Walk to:** St. Mary's Churchyard (10-minute walk)
- **End at:** St. Mary's Church (5-minute walk)

Visiting Information

- **Opening Hours:**

- Whitby Abbey: Open daily from 9:00 AM to 5:00 PM (April–October); reduced hours in winter months.
  - The Dracula Experience: Open daily from 10:00 AM to 5:00 PM (seasonal).
- **Days of Operation:**
  - Whitby Abbey: Open year-round, but may close for special events or holidays.
  - The Dracula Experience: Open year-round, though hours may vary seasonally.
- **Address:** Whitby Abbey, Abbey Lane, Whitby, YO22 4JT, UK
- **Costs:**
  - Whitby Abbey: £10 for adults, £5 for children (5-16), free for children under 5.
  - The Dracula Experience: £6 for adults, £4 for children.
- **Accessibility:**
  - Whitby Abbey has some areas that are accessible for visitors with mobility issues, but the abbey itself is on a hill, and visitors with limited mobility may find the steep walk challenging.
  - The Dracula Experience is wheelchair accessible.
- **Best Times to Visit:** The best time to visit is spring or autumn when the weather is more

moderate and the crowds are fewer. Summer can be busy with tourists.

- **What to Bring:** Comfortable shoes for walking, especially if visiting the 199 Steps or walking up to the abbey. Bring a jacket as the weather can be unpredictable near the sea.

Literary Festivals & Events:

- **Whitby Goth Weekend (April and October):** A celebration of all things Gothic, this festival brings together fans of horror, Gothic fiction, and Stoker's *Dracula*. The weekend features music, literature, and themed events, making it a perfect time for literary tourism.
- **Dracula Society Events:** Throughout the year, the Dracula Society holds special events, including talks, readings, and gatherings in Whitby. Check their website for more information on dates and activities.

Nearby Attractions

- **Whitby Museum:** Located in Pannett Park, this museum offers a deeper dive into Whitby's history and features exhibits on the town's maritime past, fossils, and Victorian life.

- **⊠ e Captain Cook Memorial Museum:** A small museum dedicated to the life of Captain James Cook, who spent time in Whitby before his famous voyages. The museum gives insight into the town's maritime history.
- **Whitby Beach:** A short walk from the town center, Whitby's beach offers the chance to relax after exploring the town's literary sites. The beach is known for its charming atmosphere, with plenty of cafes and restaurants to enjoy.

Further Reading

- *Dracula* by Bram Stoker: The novel that immortalized Whitby in the Gothic literary canon. It's essential reading for anyone interested in the town's literary connections.
- *The Complete Guide to the Dracula Experience* by David A. Sutton: A detailed exploration of Stoker's *Dracula*, with a focus on the locations and inspirations behind the novel.
- *Bram Stoker: A Biography* by Barbara Belford: A biography of the author, detailing his life and the inspirations behind his greatest work.
- *The Real Dracula: Bram Stoker and Whitby* by George Parker: A book that delves into the connections between Whitby and Stoker's

Dracula, offering historical context and insights into the town's influence on the novel.

Whitby remains a must-visit destination for fans of Gothic literature and those interested in the life and works of Bram Stoker. The town's eerie beauty and rich literary history continue to inspire writers, readers, and tourists alike.

Yorkshire
(Ted Hughes and
Sylvia Plath)

Background Information

Ted Hughes (1930–1998) was one of England's greatest poets, known for his vivid depictions of nature and mythology. Born in Mytholmroyd, West Yorkshire, Hughes found inspiration in the rugged landscapes of the Calder Valley. His poetry, including works like Crow and Birthday Letters, reflects the raw power of the natural world.

Sylvia Plath (1932–1963), an American poet and novelist, was married to Hughes and is also closely associated with Yorkshire. Her grave in Heptonstall has become a site of literary pilgrimage. Plath's work, including The Bell Jar and Ariel, reveals a deep engagement with personal struggle and the natural landscape.

Literary Quotes

Ted Hughes: "The wolf sang, the wind was wild, the sky was full of birds." – The Iron Man (1968) "What happens in the heart simply happens." – Birthday Letters (1998)

Sylvia Plath: "I am silver and exact. I have no preconceptions." – Mirror (1961) "Out of the ash / I rise with my red hair / And I eat men like air." – Lady Lazarus (1965)

Key Literary Sites in Yorkshire

Hughes' Birthplace – Mytholmroyd
- **Location:** Mytholmroyd, West Yorkshire

- **Description:** The childhood home of Ted Hughes, where he developed his deep connection with nature and the Pennine landscape.
- **Must-See Features:**
  - Plaques marking his birthplace.
  - The surrounding countryside that influenced his poetry.

Heptonstall Church & Sylvia Plath's Grave
- **Location:** Heptonstall, West Yorkshire
- **Description:** The resting place of Sylvia Plath, visited by admirers and literary enthusiasts.
- **Must-See Features:**
  - Plath's simple yet powerful gravestone.
  - The historic church ruins nearby.

Lumb Bank (⊠ e Arvon Foundation)
- **Location:** Heptonstall, near Hebden Bridge
- **Description:** Formerly Ted Hughes' home, now a renowned writing retreat.
- **Must-See Features:**
  - The surrounding valley that inspired Hughes' poetry.
  - Writing courses and literary events hosted by the Arvon Foundation.

Stubbing Wharf Pub

- **Location:** Hebden Bridge, West Yorkshire
- **Description:** A pub famously associated with Ted Hughes, mentioned in his poem "Stubbing Wharfe."
- **Must-See Features:**
  - Riverside location with views of the Calder Valley.
  - A historic setting linked to Hughes' literary life.

☒ e Calder Valley & Hardcastle Crags
- **Location:** Near Hebden Bridge, West Yorkshire
- **Description:** A scenic woodland area that influenced Hughes' poetic imagery.
- **Must-See Features:**
  - Walking trails through dramatic landscapes.
  - Gibson Mill, a 19th-century cotton mill in the heart of the valley.

Short Walks

Ted Hughes Literary Walk
- **Start: Mytholmroyd** (Ted Hughes' birthplace)
- **Walk to: Stubbing Wharf Pub** (20-minute walk)
- **Continue to: Hardcastle Crags** (40-minute walk)
- **End at: Heptonstall Church & Sylvia Plath's Grave** (30-minute walk)

Visiting Information

- **Opening Hours:**
    - o Heptonstall Church: Open daily.
    - o Lumb Bank (Arvon Foundation): Open for scheduled retreats and events.
    - o Hardcastle Crags: Open year-round.
- **Entry Fees:**
  o Heptonstall Church: Free.
  o Hardcastle Crags: Free entry; parking fees apply.
- **Accessibility:**
  o Heptonstall Church has uneven pathways.
  o Hardcastle Crags features some steep trails.
- **Best Time to Visit:** Spring and autumn for ideal walking conditions and fewer crowds.
- **What to Bring:** Walking boots, a notebook for inspiration, and a copy of Birthday Letters or Ariel.

Literary Festivals & Events

- **Ted Hughes Festival** (October, Mytholmroyd): Celebrates the poet's legacy with readings, talks, and workshops.
- **Sylvia Plath Memorial Readings** (Annual, Heptonstall): A gathering of fans and poets to honor Plath's work.

- **Arvon Foundation Writing Courses** (Year-Round, Lumb Bank): Residential retreats for aspiring writers.

Nearby Attractions

- **Brontë Parsonage Museum** (Haworth): The home of the Brontë sisters, a short drive from Heptonstall.
- **Piece Hall** (Halifax): A historic market square featuring literary events and bookshops.
- **Hebden Bridge:** A vibrant town with independent bookshops, arts venues, and a strong literary culture.

Further Reading

- *Crow* by Ted Hughes
- *Birthday Letters* by Ted Hughes
- *The Bell Jar* by Sylvia Plath
- *Ariel* by Sylvia Plath
- *Ted Hughes: The Unauthorised Life* by Jonathan Bate
- *Red Comet: The Short Life and Blazing Art of Sylvia Plath* by Heather Clark

Exploring Yorkshire through the works of Ted Hughes and Sylvia Plath offers a journey into the raw beauty of nature, poetic intensity, and the landscapes that shaped two of the 20th century's most celebrated writers.

Conclusion

England's literary heritage is woven into its landscapes, cities, and historic landmarks, offering an immersive experience for readers and travelers alike. From the rolling hills of the Lake District that inspired Wordsworth to the shadowy ruins of Whitby Abbey that shaped *Dracula*, each site tells a story beyond the pages of a book.

Walking the same paths as Shakespeare in Stratford-upon-Avon, visiting Dickens' London, or stepping into the world of Austen in Bath brings literature to life in an unparalleled way.

These fifteen sites are more than just places. They are windows into the minds of the great writers who shaped English literature. Whether you are a lifelong reader or a curious traveler, exploring these literary landmarks deepens your connection to the stories and authors that continue to inspire generations. England is not just a land of history; it is a land of stories waiting to be rediscovered.

◆◆◆

Yearning to delve into the mysteries of the English realm? Skip the tourist traps and unearth new ways to delight in its legendary landscape.

Start reading England: Cultured, Classic, and Charming and start your adventure today!

Author's Website
Universal Links

◆◆◆

Thank You!

Thank you so much for enjoying England's Literary Landmarks. If you've enjoyed the book, please consider leaving a review to help other readers find this resource.

Giving a review to an author is like the applause at the end of a concert, and authors greatly appreciate them!

◆◆◆

If you would like to get updates, sneak previews, sales, and FREE STUFF, please sign up for my newsletter.

Monthly Newsletter Signup

See all the books available through Green Dragon
Publishing at
http://www.greendragonartist.com/books

About the Author

Christy Nicholas writes under several pen names, including Emeline Rhys, CN Jackson, and Rowan Dillon. She is an author, artist, and accountant. After she failed to become an airline pilot, she quit her ceaseless pursuit of careers that began with the letter 'A' and decided to concentrate on her writing. Since she has Project Completion Compulsion, she is one of the few authors with no unfinished novels.

Christy has her hands in many crafts, including digital art, beaded jewelry, writing, and photography. In real life, she's a CPA, but having grown up with art all around her (her mother, grandmother, and great-grandmother are/were all artists), it sort of infected her, as it were.

She wants to expose the incredible beauty in this world, hidden beneath the everyday grime of familiarity and habit, and share it with others. She uses characters out of time and places infused with magic and myth, writing magical realism stories in both historical fantasy and time travel flavors.

Social Media Links:

Blog: www.GreenDragonArtist.net
Website: www.GreenDragonArtist.com
Facebook: www.facebook.com/greendragonauthor
Instagram: www.instagram.com/greendragonartist9
TikTok: www.tiktok.com/@greendragonauthor

www.ingramcontent.com/pod-product-compliance
Ingram Content Group UK Ltd.
Pitfield, Milton Keynes, MK11 3LW, UK
UKHW011828220225
455358UK00017B/559

9 798230 671879